W9-BOO-808

by Michael Sandler

Consultant: Norries Wilson
Head Football Coach
Columbia University

PUBLISHING

New York, New York

Credits

Cover and Title Page, © Paul Jasienski/Getty Images, David Sherman/NBAE via Getty Images, and R1/Alamy; 4, © Bradenton Herald/MCT/Landov; 5, © Nell Redmond/UPI/Landov; 6, © Al Messerschmidt/Getty Images; 7, © Jed Jacobsohn/Getty Images; 9T, Courtesy of the Fitzgerald family; 9B, Courtesy of the Fitzgerald family; 10, Courtesy of the Minnesota Vikings; 11, © Eric Miller/Reuters/Landov; 12, Courtesy of the University of Pittsburgh; 13, © Jason Cohn/Icon SMI; 14, © Ai Wire/Newscom; 15, © AP Images/Tom Hood; 16, © AP Images/Paul Connors; 17, © Gary Hershon/Reuters/Landov; 18, © Art Foxall/UPI/Landov; 19, © David Sherman/NBAE via Getty Images; 20, © Hugh Gentry/Reuters/Landov; 21, © Hugh Gentry/Reuters/Landov; 22L, © MCT/Newscom; 22R, © Icon Sports Media.

Publisher: Kenn Goin
Senior Editor: Lisa Wiseman
Creative Director: Spencer Brinker
Photo Researcher: Omni-Photo Communications, Inc.
Design: Dawn Beard Creative

Library of Congress Cataloging-in-Publication Data

Sandler, Michael, 1965–
  Larry Fitzgerald / by Michael Sandler ; consultant, Norries Wilson.
    p. cm. — (Football heroes making a difference)
  Includes bibliographical references and index.
  ISBN-13: 978-1-936087-58-7 (library binding)
  ISBN-10: 1-936087-58-8 (library binding)
  1. Fitzgerald, Larry, 1983–Juvenile literature. 2. Football players—United States—Biography—Juvenile literature. I. Wilson, Norries. II. Title.
  GV939.F55S36 2010
  796.33092—dc22
  [B]
                                                                    Z0064823
                            2009028305

For more information, write to Bearport Publishing Company, Inc., 45 West 21st St, Suite 3B, New York, New York 10010. Printed in the United States of America in North Mankato, Minnesota.

072011
071111CGC

10 9 8 7 6 5 4 3 2

CONTENTS

Laughing No Longer

For as long as people could remember, the Arizona Cardinals were one of the NFL's worst teams. Year after year, they lost game after game. Fans often joked about the team's losing ways.

During the 2008–2009 season, however, people finally stopped laughing. First, a winning record earned the Cardinals a playoff spot. Then two big wins sent the team into the **NFC Championship Game**. With one more victory— over the Philadelphia Eagles—Arizona would reach its first ever Super Bowl.

Earlier in the season, Philadelphia had beaten the Cardinals, 48–20. Could Arizona do better this time? In order to do so, the team needed a great performance from its star—**wide receiver** Larry Fitzgerald.

Arizona was finally giving fans a reason to cheer.

To reach the NFC Championship Game in January 2009, the Cardinals beat the Carolina Panthers and the Atlanta Falcons. Larry scored touchdowns in both wins.

Larry (far left) leaps to catch a pass against the Carolina Panthers during the playoff game.

Three Touchdowns

Throughout the game against Philadelphia on January 18, 2009, Larry did his best to come through for the team. In the first quarter, quarterback Kurt Warner found him for an easy touchdown pass.

Kurt and Larry struck again in the second quarter. Kurt launched a bomb deep downfield. Larry raced past Eagles **safety** Quintin Demps to grab the long pass—touchdown number two!

Then, just before halftime, Larry pulled down an incredible third touchdown pass to give the Cardinals a 24–6 lead. Arizona held on to win 32–25. Thanks to Larry, the team was headed to the Super Bowl!

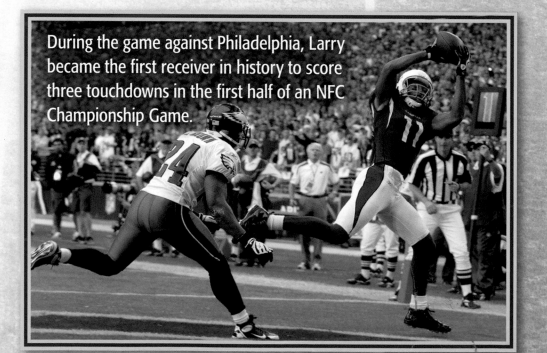

During the game against Philadelphia, Larry became the first receiver in history to score three touchdowns in the first half of an NFC Championship Game.

Larry celebrates Arizona's win against the Eagles.

In the win against Philadelphia, Larry caught nine passes for 152 yards (139 m). Altogether, he collected 419 yards (383 m) in the Cardinals' first three playoff games—an NFL playoff record.

Looking to Mom

The hard work and **passion** Larry showed in the big win against the Eagles was something he learned about from his mother, Carol. She was his **role model**. He even kept her photo in his wallet. Each day before the championship game, Larry looked at it.

Growing up in Minneapolis, Minnesota, Larry had seen the effort she put into her job. Carol worked for the Minnesota Department of Health. She helped people learn how to deal with diseases such as **cancer** and **AIDS**. Helping others was her passion. From his mom, Larry learned to put his all into everything he did, especially his favorite sport—football.

Larry was born on August 31, 1983, in Minneapolis, Minnesota.

Larry's family (left to right): his brother, Marcus; his dad, Larry Sr.; Larry; and his mom, Carol (center front)

Larry, in his high school football uniform, with his parents

Larry loved playing football so much that as a child he even slept with his football.

Learning the Game

Larry's hard-working ways came from his mom, but his love of football came from his father. Larry Fitzgerald, Sr., had been a talented college player. From a young age, Larry showed similar skills. He tried every position from **linebacker** to **cornerback**, but by high school he ended up as a wide receiver. Coaches loved his "sticky" hands. He never seemed to drop a ball.

In high school, Larry also worked as a ball boy for the NFL's Minnesota Vikings. He folded towels for the players and helped out during **drills**. His eyes were always focused on the Vikings' receivers, especially Cris Carter and Randy Moss. He watched how they caught the ball. He tried his best to copy their moves.

Larry working as a ball boy for the Minnesota Vikings

Minneapolis receiver Cris Carter (right) was one of Larry's childhood idols.

Larry's father could tell right away that his son would be a special football player. He didn't tell Larry, though. "I didn't want it to go to his head," said Larry's father.

Handling Loss

After high school, Larry went on to college at the University of Pittsburgh. He had a successful first football season, but near the end of freshman year, something terrible happened. His mother, who was battling cancer, died.

The loss hit Larry hard. To deal with the pain, he threw himself even more into the sport that he loved. He spent days in the weight room strengthening his body. He watched hundreds of hours of different games and plays on videotape. For Larry, the time spent preparing for the upcoming football season was like **therapy**. It helped him handle the pain of his mother's death.

Larry (right) had 10 catches for 103 yards (94 m) against Texas A&M in his second college game.

Larry felt that continuing to play football was what his mother would have wanted. "My mom always said that once she was gone, I should just keep living as if she was still there," recalled Larry.

Becoming the Best

Larry's hard work paid off during his second year at Pittsburgh. Game after game, the receiver left opposing **defenders** feeling shaken. When he went up for the ball, he was fearless. No one could stop him. No one could cover him. People considered him the nation's top pass catcher.

When the football season ended, Larry decided he was ready for **pro** football. He entered the 2004 NFL **draft** after just two years of college football. The Arizona Cardinals proved he had made the right decision. They chose Larry with the third pick in the draft.

At Pittsburgh, Larry (right) set a college record for the most games in a row with at least one touchdown catch—18.

Larry, with Arizona's coach Dennis
Green (right), on draft day

04

Dennis Green was thrilled when the Cardinals
drafted Larry. He already knew Larry well.
Dennis had been Minnesota's coach when
Larry was a ball boy for the Vikings.

Coming Through for the Cardinals

The Cardinals hoped for big things from their new receiver. Larry didn't disappoint them. In his **rookie** season, he made 58 catches for 780 yards (713 m). Coaches noticed his special knack for making the toughest catches. His timing was perfect. He knew just when to jump to reach a highly thrown ball.

Over the next few seasons, Larry became one of the league's **dominant** receivers. In 2008, he did what many people thought was impossible—he helped Arizona achieve a winning record. Then, along with Kurt Warner, he led the team into the playoffs and the Cardinals' first ever Super Bowl.

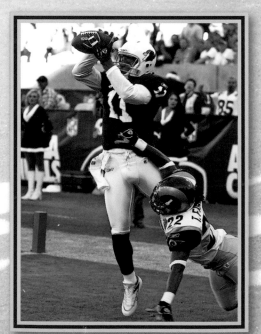

Larry (#11) pulls down a touchdown pass during his rookie season.

Larry's 64-yard (59-m) touchdown play gave Arizona a fourth-quarter lead in Super Bowl XLIII (43).

In Super Bowl XLIII (43), Larry was at the top of his game. He made seven catches for 127 yards (116 m)—two of them for touchdowns. Yet the Cardinals lost a heartbreaker when the Pittsburgh Steelers scored a last-minute touchdown to take a 27–23 win.

Keeping the Work Alive

Larry's NFL success could never erase the pain he felt when his mother died. He kept her driver's license in his wallet so he could always look at her photo. He wore long **dreadlocks**—his mother's hairstyle—in her honor. Most important, he decided to find a way to continue the work his mother had believed in. Along with his father and his brother, Marcus, Larry set up the Carol Fitzgerald Memorial Fund. Its main goals are to teach people about cancer and AIDS, and to help those who are suffering from these serious diseases.

Larry wearing his signature dreadlocks

On the check:

10000

MINNESOTA TIMBERWOLVES
FASTBREAK
Foundation

DATE April 11ᵗʰ, 2009

PAY TO THE
ORDER OF Carol Fitzgerald Memorial Fund $ 2,500.⁰⁰

Two Thousand five Hundred Dollars   DOLLARS

Lynx foundation

Larry (right) and his father (middle) receive a check for the Carol Fitzgerald Memorial Fund.

Each year, Larry hosts a **benefit** to raise money for the Carol Fitzgerald Memorial Fund. The money goes to groups that help people with cancer and AIDS. It's also used to create programs that teach young people about both diseases.

Teaching Others

Hard work and talent helped make Larry a star. The time he spent working as a ball boy was also important. Larry learned so much from the pros he watched in his early teens. "When I was that age and could get tips from Randy Moss and Cris Carter, it was wonderful," he remembers.

In order to give other kids the same experience, he started the Larry Fitzgerald, Jr., Football Camp. At the camp, Larry teaches young teens the techniques of the game—just as Randy Moss and Cris Carter had done with him.

Larry knows that helping others means as much as playing in a Super Bowl. He calls the work he's done in his mother's memory his "biggest defining moment as a man."

After Super Bowl XLIII (43), Larry played in the 2009 **Pro Bowl**, the NFL's all-star game. Larry caught two touchdown passes to help his team win. He was named Pro Bowl **MVP**.

Larry at the Pro Bowl

Larry with his MVP trophy

The Larry File

Larry is a football hero on and off the field. Here are some highlights.

TM

- When Larry was young, his father didn't want him to play football because he was worried that Larry would get injured. Larry's mom felt otherwise and convinced her husband to let their son play.

- Larry's hobby is cooking. He's taken cooking classes for years and one of his favorite dishes to make is shish kebabs.

- The money raised by Larry's summer football camp goes to support the Carol Fitzgerald Memorial Fund.

- Larry Fitzgerald, Sr., is a sports reporter and radio host. When he reported on Super Bowl XLIII (43), it marked the first time a father had covered his own son for the NFL's biggest game.

- During the 2008–2009 playoffs, including Super Bowl XLIII (43), Larry made 30 catches for 546 yards (499 m)—an NFL record.

Glossary

AIDS (AYDZ) an often deadly disease in which the body's ability to protect itself against illness is destroyed

benefit (BEN-uh-fit) an event held to raise money for a good cause

cancer (KAN-sur) a serious, often deadly, disease that destroys parts of the body

cornerback (KOR-nur-bak) a player on defense who usually covers the other team's receivers

defenders (di-FEND-urz) players who have the job of stopping the other team from scoring

dominant (DOM-uh-nuhnt) the most powerful; the very best

draft (DRAFT) an event in which professional teams take turns choosing college players to play for them

dreadlocks (DRED-loks) a type of hairstyle in which the hair is grown long and worn in braids

drills (DRILZ) training exercises used to make players better

linebacker (LINE-bak-ur) a defensive player on the second line of defenders who makes tackles and defends passes

MVP (EM-VEE-PEE) the most valuable player

NFC Championship Game (EN-EFF-SEE CHAM-pee-uhn-ship GAME) a playoff game that decides which National Football Conference (NFC) team will go to the Super Bowl

passion (PASH-uhn) very strong feelings about something; a strong interest in something

pro (PROH) professional; an athlete who gets paid to play a sport

Pro Bowl (PROH BOHL) the yearly all-star game for the season's best NFL players

role model (ROHL MOD-uhl) a person whose behavior or success is held up as an example or inspiration

rookie (RUK-ee) a first-year player

safety (SAYF-tee) a defensive player who lines up farther back than other defensive players

therapy (THER-uh-pee) treatment for a medical or emotional problem

wide receiver (WIDE ri-SEE-vur) a player whose job it is to catch passes

Bibliography

Craig, Mark. "Larry Fitzgerald, Jr.: A Long Way from Home." *Star Tribune* (Minneapolis) (January 26, 2009).

The New York Times

St. Paul Pioneer Press

Sports Illustrated

Read More

Gilbert, Sara. *The History of the Arizona Cardinals.* Mankato, MN: Creative Education (2005).

Grabowski, John. *Larry Fitzgerald.* Broomall, PA: Mason Crest (2009).

Sandler, Michael. *Kurt Warner and the St. Louis Rams: Super Bowl XXXIV.* New York: Bearport (2008).

Learn More Online

To learn more about Larry Fitzgerald and the Arizona Cardinals, visit
www.bearportpublishing.com/FootballHeroes

Index